FAVORITE BRAND NAME

KRAFT
Diabetic
Choices

Publications International, Ltd.

Favorite Brand Name Recipes at www.fbnr.com

Recipe Development: Kraft Kitchens
Recipe Nutrition: Kraft Foods Staff Registered Dietitians
Project Coordination: Kraft Diabetic Partnership

Photography: Stephen Hamilton Photographics, Inc.
Photographers: Stephen Hamilton, Tate Hunt
Prop Stylist: Paula Walters
Food Stylists: Josephine Orba, Mary-Helen Steindler
Assistant Food Stylist: Susie Skoog

Pictured on the front cover *(Top to bottom):* Sunny Orange Delight *(page 72)* and Spicy Asian Shrimp Salad *(page 26)*.

Inset Photo on front cover: Mocha Pudding Parfaits *(page 90)*.

Pictured on the back cover *(Top to bottom):* Bacon and Creamy Fettuccine *(page 40)*, JELL-O® 'n Juicy Fruit Parfait *(page 86)* and Vegetable Turkey Pockets *(page 8)*.

Nutrition Analysis: Nutrition information is provided for all of the recipes in this publication. Each analysis is based on the food items in the ingredient list, except ingredients labeled as "optional" or "as desired." When more than one ingredient choice is listed, the first ingredient is used for analysis. Nutrition claims are based on criteria set forth in government regulations for nutrition labeling of foods. Exchange calculations are based on *Exchange Lists for Meal Planning*, © 1995, the American Diabetes Association, Inc. and The American Dietetic Association.

Contents

Visit us on the web at
www.kraftdiabeticchoices.com

Introduction

Welcome to *Diabetic Choices*—an exciting new cookbook brought to you by the Kraft family of brands. Thanks to the easy and delicious recipes in this book, you and your whole family can enjoy healthful meals together.

Have a Plan

Be the best you can be now and in the future by creating an action plan to control your diabetes. Meet with a registered dietitian or a certified diabetes educator to develop a meal plan and exercise routine that is right for you. A good strategy will allow you to enjoy food and lead a fulfilling life.

Stay Active

Regular exercise can help improve body weight and blood glucose and may lower blood cholesterol levels. Exercise may also reduce your risk of high blood pressure and heart disease. Health experts advise adults to get 30 minutes of exercise daily.

You Have Choices

Fortunately, restrictive diets are a thing of the past. This doesn't mean you can eat anything you want whenever you want, but with an understanding of food exchange lists and carbohydrate counting, your meal choices are plentiful. Eating a balanced diet with a variety of foods in moderate amounts makes sense for everyone—not just for people living with diabetes.

Help Yourself

Learn as much as you can about diabetes. The more you know, the better you will feel. A positive attitude plus support from family and friends can go a long way.

Recipe Nutrition Know-How

Recipes in this book were developed according to nutrition recommendations set forth by the American Diabetes Association. Each recipe lists nutrition information per serving for calories, fat, carbohydrate and protein. Many recipes contain good-for-you nutrients, like fiber, vitamin A, vitamin C, calcium and iron. Exchange values are also given so you can see how a recipe can fit into your eating plan.

Some recipes are highlighted with special symbols, indicating they are low in fat or calories or good sources of fiber or calcium.

 Low Fat: contains 3 grams or less of fat per reference amount*

 Contains Fiber: contains 2½ grams or more of fiber per reference amount

 Good Source of Calcium: contains 10% or more of the daily value for calcium per reference amount

 Low Calorie: contains 40 calories or less per reference amount

Check Us Out!

Visit us at www.kraftdiabeticchoices.com to get more great recipes and nutrition information. You are just a click away from meal-planning tips, seasonal features, recipe contests and links to other websites about diabetes. Let us show you how easy it is to rely on Kraft for food products that turn your meal plan into delicious results your whole family will enjoy.

* Reference amount is specified by the government for food categories and is the basis for serving size.

Diabetic Choices

Lunch on the Run

Whether you're eating at home or on the go, you'll love this yummy assortment of great-tasting sandwiches.

Vegetable Turkey Pockets

Prep: 20 minutes plus refrigerating

¼ cup SEVEN SEAS FREE Ranch Fat Free Dressing
¼ cup KRAFT Mayo Light Mayonnaise
1½ cups LOUIS RICH Oven Roasted Turkey Breast strips
½ cup chopped cucumber
½ cup shredded carrot
1 small tomato, chopped
1 teaspoon dried basil leaves, crushed
2 pita breads, cut in half

MIX dressing, mayo, turkey, cucumber, carrot, tomato and basil. Refrigerate.

FILL pita bread halves with turkey mixture.

Makes 4 servings

Nutrition Information Per Serving: 200 calories, 6g total fat, 1g saturated fat, 20mg cholesterol, 870mg sodium, 27g carbohydrate, 2g dietary fiber, 10g protein

80% daily value vitamin A, 10% daily value vitamin C

Exchange: 1 Starch, 1 Carbohydrate, 1 Meat (L)

My Hero
Prep: 10 minutes

½ cup KRAFT Mayo Fat Free Mayonnaise Dressing
¼ cup KRAFT FREE Italian Fat Free Dressing
3 cups shredded lettuce
1 loaf (about 1 pound) French bread, split in half
    lengthwise
1 package (8 ounces) OSCAR MAYER FREE Fat Free
    Bologna
1 package (6 ounces) OSCAR MAYER FREE DELI-THIN
    Oven Roasted Fat Free Turkey Breast
2 medium tomatoes, thinly sliced
6 KRAFT FREE Singles Nonfat Process Cheese Product
1 medium green pepper, thinly sliced

MIX dressings.

TOSS lettuce with ¼ cup of the dressing mixture; set aside.

BRUSH cut surfaces of bread with remaining dressing mixture. Top bottom half of bread with lettuce mixture, meat, tomatoes, process cheese product and green pepper; cover with top half of bread. Cut sandwich into 8 pieces to serve.

Makes 8 servings

Nutrition Information Per Serving: 250 calories, 3g total fat, 0.5g saturated fat, 20mg cholesterol, 1320mg sodium, 40g carbohydrate, 3g dietary fiber, 16g protein

10% daily value vitamin A, 30% daily value vitamin C, 15% daily value calcium

Exchange: 2½ Starch, 1 Meat (VL)

My Hero

Ham Sandwich with Nectarine Salsa

Prep: 10 minutes

1 nectarine, coarsely chopped
2 tablespoons KRAFT Mayo Fat Free Mayonnaise
    Dressing *or* MIRACLE WHIP FREE Nonfat Dressing
2 tablespoons chopped sweet onion
1 tablespoon chopped fresh cilantro
½ teaspoon fresh lime juice
    Dash ground red pepper
3 pita bread halves
3 lettuce leaves
1 package (5.5 ounces) LOUIS RICH CARVING BOARD
    Thin Carved Honey Glazed Ham

MIX nectarine, dressing, onion, cilantro, lime juice and red pepper to make salsa.

FILL each pita bread half with lettuce, 3 ham slices and ⅓ of the salsa.

Makes 3 servings

FAT

Nutrition Information Per Serving: 150 calories, 1g total fat, 0g saturated fat, 25mg cholesterol, 830mg sodium, 26g carbohydrate, 2g dietary fiber, 10g protein

Exchange: 1 Starch, ½ Fruit, 1 Meat (VL)

Vegetable Pita Pockets

Prep: 15 minutes

½ cup chopped cucumber
½ cup chopped carrot
 2 tablespoons KRAFT LIGHT DONE RIGHT Ranch
      Reduced Fat Dressing
 1 pita bread, cut in half
½ small tomato, sliced
 2 KRAFT 2% Milk Singles Process Cheese Food with
      Added Calcium, cut in half
    Lettuce

MIX cucumber, carrot and dressing.

SPOON cucumber mixture into pita bread halves. Fill with tomato slices, 2% Milk Singles and lettuce.

Makes 1 serving

CALCIUM

Nutrition Information Per Serving: 380 calories, 14g total fat, 4.5g saturated fat, 30mg cholesterol, 1230mg sodium, 50g carbohydrate, 5g dietary fiber, 16g protein

100% daily value vitamin A, 35% daily value vitamin C, 50% daily value calcium

Exchange: 2½ Starch, 2 Vegetable, 1 Meat (MF), 1 Fat

Mediterranean Wrap Sandwich

Prep: 10 minutes plus refrigerating

½ cup MIRACLE WHIP FREE Nonfat Dressing *or* KRAFT
    Mayo Fat Free Mayonnaise Dressing
½ teaspoon dried oregano leaves
½ teaspoon garlic powder
8 flour tortillas (8 inch)
2 packages (5.5 ounces each) LOUIS RICH CARVING
    BOARD Oven Roasted Turkey Breast
1 cup cucumber strips
1 red pepper, cut into strips

MIX dressing and seasonings. Spread onto tortillas.

TOP with turkey, cucumber and red pepper; roll up. Wrap
in plastic wrap. Refrigerate until ready to serve.

Makes 8 servings

Variation: Prepare as directed. Cut rolls into 1-inch pieces for
bite-size snacks or appetizers.

Nutrition Information Per Serving: 220 calories, 4.5g total fat,
1g saturated fat, 20mg cholesterol, 840mg sodium, 32g carbohydrate,
2g dietary fiber, 13g protein

Exchange: 2 Starch, 1 Meat (VL), ½ Fat

Mediterranean Wrap Sandwich

Hummus Veggie Pockets

Prep: 10 minutes

1 can (15½ ounces) chick peas, drained
⅓ cup KRAFT House Italian Dressing
¼ teaspoon cracked pepper
4 whole wheat pita breads, cut in half
½ cup shredded carrot

PLACE chick peas in food processor container with steel blade attached; cover. Process until almost smooth, scraping down side of container as needed.

ADD dressing and pepper. Process until smooth.

FILL each pita bread half with about 3 tablespoons hummus mixture. Sprinkle with carrot.

Makes 4 servings

Tips: Prepare as directed, adding green or red pepper strips, sliced cucumber or zucchini, chopped tomato and shredded lettuce.

Serve as a dip for cut-up vegetables or bread sticks.

Refrigerate leftover hummus in a covered container.

FIBER

Nutrition Information Per Serving: 280 calories, 6g total fat, 1g saturated fat, 0mg cholesterol, 590mg sodium, 50g carbohydrate, 8g dietary fiber, 9g protein

70% daily value vitamin A, 15 % daily value iron

Exchange: 3 Starch, 1 Fat

Salsa Turkey Grill

Prep: 5 minutes   Cook: 5 minutes

2 slices bread
1 KRAFT FREE Singles Nonfat Process Cheese Product
1 tablespoon TACO BELL HOME ORIGINALS Thick 'N
    Chunky Salsa
2 slices LOUIS RICH CARVING BOARD Oven Roasted
    Turkey Breast
1 teaspoon margarine, softened

TOP 1 bread slice with process cheese product, salsa, turkey and second bread slice.

SPREAD outside of sandwich with margarine.

COOK in nonstick skillet on medium heat until lightly browned on both sides.

Makes 1 serving

Taco Bell® and Home Originals® are registered trademarks owned and licensed by Taco Bell Corporation.

CALCIUM

Nutrition Information Per Serving: 250 calories, 6g total fat, 1.5g saturated fat, 25mg cholesterol, 1250mg sodium, 29g carbohydrate, 1g dietary fiber, 18g protein

100% daily value vitamin A, 20% daily value calcium, 10% daily value iron

Exchange: 2 Starch, 2 Meat (VL), ½ Fat

Club Calzone

Prep: 15 minutes   Bake: 12 minutes

1 can (10 ounces) refrigerated pizza crust
¼ cup KRAFT 100% Grated Parmesan Cheese
1 cup KRAFT 2% Milk Shredded Reduced Fat
　　Mozzarella Cheese
¼ cup chopped green pepper
1 package (9 or 10 ounces) OSCAR MAYER *or* LOUIS
　　RICH FREE Fat Free Turkey or Ham

UNROLL pizza crust on lightly greased cookie sheet. Stretch crust to form 15×10-inch rectangle; sprinkle with Parmesan cheese.

LAYER mozzarella cheese, green pepper and sliced meat down center of crust.

FOLD crust over meat; pinch all edges to seal. Make small cuts across top to vent.

BAKE at 425°F for 12 minutes or until browned. Remove from cookie sheet; cool slightly on wire rack before serving.

Makes 4 servings

CALCIUM

Nutrition Information Per Serving: 330 calories, 8g total fat, 40mg cholesterol, 1530mg sodium, 36g carbohydrate, 0g dietary fiber, 27g protein

30% daily value calcium

Exchange: 2½ Starch, 2 Meat (L)

Club Calzone

Diabetic Choices

Salads for Supper

Make your suppers super with this snazzy selection of main-dish salads.

Black Bean and Mango Chicken Salad

Prep: 10 minutes plus refrigerating

1 can (16 ounces) black beans, drained, rinsed
1 package (10 ounces) frozen corn, thawed
1 cup chopped ripe mango
½ pound boneless skinless chicken breasts, grilled, cut up
½ cup chopped red pepper
⅓ cup chopped fresh cilantro
⅓ cup chopped red onion
¼ cup lime juice
1 envelope GOOD SEASONS Italian Salad Dressing Mix

TOSS all ingredients in large bowl. Refrigerate.

SERVE with baked tortilla chips, if desired.

Makes 4 servings

Nutrition Information Per Serving: 250 calories, 2.5g total fat, 0.5g saturated fat, 35mg cholesterol, 990mg sodium, 40g carbohydrate, 7g dietary fiber, 20g protein

60% daily value vitamin A, 100% daily value vitamin C

Exchange: 2½ Carbohydrate, 1½ Meat (VL)

Grilled Steak Salad

Prep: 15 minutes   Grill: 14 minutes

¾ pound beef sirloin steak, ½ to ¾ inch thick
  1 teaspoon cracked pepper
10 cups torn romaine lettuce *or* 1 package (10 ounces)
    mixed salad greens
  1 beefsteak or other large tomato, cut into wedges
  1 small zucchini, sliced
½ cup slivered red onion
½ cup KRAFT LIGHT DONE RIGHT Thousand Island
    Reduced Fat Dressing

PLACE steak on grill over medium-hot coals. Sprinkle with pepper. Grill 5 to 7 minutes on each side to medium doneness.

CUT steak across grain into thin slices. Arrange all ingredients except dressing on individual plates. Serve with dressing.

Makes 4 servings

Tip: This recipe is a perfect way to use leftover cooked steak or roast beef.

Nutrition Information Per Serving: 230 calories, 9g total fat, 2.5g saturated fat, 55mg cholesterol, 370mg sodium, 15g carbohydrate, 4g dietary fiber, 22g protein

80% daily value vitamin A, 80% daily value vitamin C

Exchange: 3 Vegetable, 2 Meat (L), 1 Fat

Grilled Steak Salad

Creamy Ranch & Parmesan Chicken Salad

Prep: 10 minutes   **Cook:** 10 minutes

4 boneless skinless chicken breast halves
    (about 1¼ pounds), cut into strips
1 cup KRAFT FREE Ranch Fat Free Dressing, divided
½ cup KRAFT FREE Nonfat Grated Topping
1 package (10 ounces) salad greens
1 cup cherry tomatoes
1 cup seasoned croutons
1 red, yellow or green pepper, cut into strips

TOSS chicken with ¼ cup of the dressing in large bowl; coat with grated topping.

SPRAY large skillet with no stick cooking spray. Add chicken; cook and stir on medium heat 10 minutes or until cooked through.

TOSS chicken, greens, tomatoes, croutons and pepper lightly with remaining ¾ cup dressing.

Makes 6 servings

Variation: Prepare as directed, substituting KRAFT Peppercorn Ranch Dressing or KRAFT FREE Peppercorn Ranch Fat Free Dressing for Ranch Dressing.

Nutrition Information Per Serving: 250 calories, 4g total fat, 1.5g saturated fat, 60mg cholesterol, 790mg sodium, 28g carbohydrate, 4g dietary fiber, 25g protein

45% daily value vitamin A, 60% daily value vitamin C

Exchange: 1½ Starch, 1 Vegetable, 3 Meat (VL)

Greek Chicken Salad

Prep: 10 minutes   Cook: 10 minutes

1 cup KRAFT FREE Italian Fat Free Dressing
1 teaspoon dried oregano leaves, crushed
1 pound boneless skinless chicken breasts, cut into strips
1 package (10 ounces) salad greens
1 package (4 ounces) ATHENOS Crumbled Feta Cheese
3 plum tomatoes, sliced
½ cucumber, seeded, sliced and quartered
1 cup pitted ripe olives
½ cup thinly sliced red onion

MIX dressing and oregano. Cook chicken in 3 tablespoons of the dressing mixture in large skillet on medium heat 10 minutes or until cooked through.

TOSS remaining ingredients except chicken with remaining dressing mixture. Place on serving platter. Arrange chicken over greens mixture.

Makes 6 servings

Nutrition Information Per Serving: 180 calories, 7g total fat, 3.5g saturated fat, 40mg cholesterol, 880mg sodium, 13g carbohydrate, 3g dietary fiber, 17g protein

45% daily value vitamin A, 40% daily value vitamin C

Exchange: 1 Vegetable, ½ Carbohydrate, 2 Meat (L)

Spicy Asian Shrimp Salad

Prep: 15 minutes

6 cups shredded romaine lettuce *or* napa cabbage
2 cups pea pods (about 6 ounces)
1 can (15 ounces) baby corn, drained
½ pound medium shrimp, cleaned, cooked
1 red pepper, cut into thin strips
½ cup KRAFT LIGHT DONE RIGHT CATALINA Reduced
    Fat Dressing
1 tablespoon soy sauce
½ to 1 teaspoon hot pepper sauce

TOSS all ingredients in large bowl.

Makes 4 servings

Variations: Prepare as directed, substituting 2 cooked boneless skinless chicken breast halves, sliced, for shrimp.

Prepare as directed, substituting 1 cup frozen corn, thawed, for baby corn.

Nutrition Information Per Serving: 200 calories, 6g total fat, 0.5g saturated fat, 110mg cholesterol, 1020mg sodium, 21g carbohydrate, 5g dietary fiber, 16g protein

100% daily value vitamin A, 100% daily value vitamin C

Exchange: 2 Vegetable, 1 Carbohydrate, 2 Meat (L)

Top to bottom: Sunny Orange Delight (page 72), Spicy Asian Shrimp Salad

Bistro Chicken Pasta Salad

Prep: 25 minutes

2 cups cooked penne pasta
1 cup quartered cherry tomatoes
1 package (4 ounces) ATHENOS Crumbled Feta Cheese
½ cup prepared GOOD SEASONS Italian Salad
    Dressing for Fat Free Dressing
⅓ cup lightly packed fresh basil leaves, cut into strips
¼ cup chopped red onion
¼ cup chopped sun-dried tomatoes (not oil-packed)
2 boneless skinless chicken breasts halves, grilled or
    broiled, cut into ¼-inch slices

TOSS all ingredients except chicken in large bowl. Spoon onto serving platter.

TOP pasta mixture with chicken. Serve warm or chilled.

Makes 4 servings

Nutrition Information Per Serving: 290 calories, 9g total fat, 4.5g saturated fat, 55mg cholesterol, 660mg sodium, 31g carbohydrate, 4g dietary fiber, 24g protein

20% daily value vitamin C

Exchange: 1½ Starch, 1 Vegetable, 2½ Meat (VL), 1 Fat

Bistro Chicken Pasta Salad

Ham & Pineapple Ranch Salad
Prep: 15 minutes

½ pound ham, julienne cut
1 can (8 ounces) pineapple chunks, drained
1 cup asparagus tips, fresh or frozen, blanched
1 package (10 ounces) salad greens
1 bottle (8 ounces) KRAFT FREE Ranch Fat Free Dressing
½ cup chow mein noodles

ARRANGE ham, pineapple and asparagus over greens.

SERVE with dressing. Sprinkle with chow mein noodles.

Makes 8 servings

Nutrition Information Per Serving: 200 calories, 8g total fat, 2.5g saturated fat, 20mg cholesterol, 930mg sodium, 23g carbohydrate, 3g dietary fiber, 9g protein

35% daily value vitamin A, 35% daily value vitamin C

Exchange: 1 Fruit, 2 Vegetable, 1 Meat (L), 1 Fat

CATALINA® Chicken Salad
Prep: 20 minutes   Cook: 8 minutes

1 pound boneless skinless chicken breasts, cut into strips
1 cup KRAFT FREE CATALINA Fat Free Dressing, divided
1 package (10 ounces) salad greens or spinach
1 cup sliced strawberries
¼ cup sliced almonds

COOK and stir chicken in ¼ cup of the dressing in large skillet on medium heat 8 minutes or until chicken is cooked through.

TOSS greens, strawberries, almonds and chicken in large bowl with remaining ¾ cup dressing.

Makes 6 servings

Nutrition Information Per Serving: 170 calories, 4g total fat, 0.5g saturated fat, 45mg cholesterol, 490mg sodium, 15g carbohydrate, 3g dietary fiber, 20g protein

60% daily value vitamin A, 40% daily value vitamin C

Exchange: 1 Carbohydrate, 2½ Meat (VL)

Chicken Berry Salad
Prep: 20 minutes

8 cups torn mixed salad greens *or* 1 package
    (10 ounces) salad greens
1 pound boneless skinless chicken breasts, cooked, cut
    into strips
2 cups assorted berries (raspberries, blueberries, sliced
    strawberries)
1 package (8 ounces) frozen sugar snap peas, thawed
¼ cup toasted pecans or slivered almonds
1 cup prepared GOOD SEASONS Italian Salad
    Dressing

TOSS all ingredients with dressing in large bowl.

Makes 6 servings

Nutrition Information Per Serving: 280 calories, 13g total fat, 2g saturated fat, 65mg cholesterol, 490mg sodium, 15g carbohydrate, 5g dietary fiber, 27g protein

50% daily value vitamin A, 50% daily value vitamin C

Exchange: 1 Carbohydrate, 3 Meat (VL), 2 Fat

Grilled Chicken Caesar Salad

Prep: 15 minutes plus marinating   Grill: 20 minutes

8 cups torn romaine lettuce
1 pound boneless skinless chicken breasts, grilled, cut
    into strips
1 cup seasoned croutons
½ cup KRAFT Shredded *or* 100% Grated Parmesan
    Cheese
¾ cup KRAFT FREE Caesar Italian Fat Free Dressing

TOSS lettuce, chicken, croutons and cheese in large salad bowl.

ADD dressing; toss to coat. Serve with fresh lemon wedges and fresh ground pepper, if desired.

Makes 4 servings

Variation: Prepare as directed, substituting 1 package (10 ounces) mixed or romaine salad greens.

Nutrition Information Per Serving: 240 calories, 7g total fat, 4g saturated fat, 55mg cholesterol, 1140mg sodium, 15g carbohydrate, 3g dietary fiber, 26g protein

Exchange: 2 Vegetable, ½ Carbohydrate, 3 Meat (L)

Grilled Chicken Caesar Salad

BBQ Ranch Chicken Salad

Prep: 15 minutes   Cook: 10 minutes

½ cup KRAFT Original Barbecue Sauce
 1 pound boneless skinless chicken breasts, cut into strips
 1 package (10 ounces) mixed salad greens
 1 large tomato, cut into wedges
½ cup sliced red onion
½ cup KRAFT LIGHT DONE RIGHT Ranch Reduced Fat
    Dressing
¼ cup crumbled blue cheese

HEAT barbecue sauce in skillet on medium-high heat. Add chicken; cook and stir until chicken is cooked through. Add additional barbecue sauce, if desired.

TOSS greens, tomato and onion in large bowl. Top with chicken. Pour dressing over greens mixture. Sprinkle with cheese.

Makes 6 servings

Variation: Place boneless skinless chicken breast halves on greased grill over medium coals. Grill 12 to 15 minutes or until cooked through, turning and brushing frequently with barbecue sauce. Slice chicken; serve over greens mixture.

Nutrition Information Per Serving: 170 calories, 7g total fat, 1.5g saturated fat, 55mg cholesterol, 370mg sodium, 6g carbohydrate, 2g dietary fiber, 20g protein

35% daily value vitamin A, 25% daily value vitamin C

Exchange: 2 Vegetable, 2 Meat (L)

Grilled Vegetable Kabob Salad

Prep: 15 minutes plus marinating   Grill: 8 minutes

1 *each* small green and red pepper, cut into 1-inch
    chunks
1 package (6 ounces) cremini *or* white mushrooms
1 small yellow summer squash, thickly sliced
1 small Vidalia *or* Walla Walla onion, cut into ¼-inch
    wedges
¾ cup KRAFT LIGHT DONE RIGHT Red Wine Vinegar
    Reduced Fat Dressing
8 cups torn assorted greens *or* 1 package (10 ounces)
    salad greens

ARRANGE vegetables alternately on 12 small skewers.
Place in large pan; brush with dressing. Let stand 30
minutes to marinate.

PLACE skewers on grill over medium-hot coals.

GRILL 6 to 8 minutes or until vegetables are tender, brushing
with dressing and turning occasionally. Place greens on
6 individual plates; top each with 2 kabobs.

Makes 6 servings

Nutrition Information Per Serving: 90 calories, 5g total fat,
0g saturated fat, 0mg cholesterol, 330mg sodium, 10g carbohydrate,
3g dietary fiber, 3g protein

45% daily value vitamin A, 60% daily value vitamin C

Exchange: 2 Vegetable, 1 Fat

Diabetic Choices

The Main Event

Your family will savor the flavor of these wonderful main dishes.

Barbecue Chicken Pizza

Prep: 15 minutes   Bake: 18 minutes

2 boneless skinless chicken breast halves
(about ½ pound), cut into thin strips
1 green pepper, cut into strips
¼ cup thinly sliced red onion
1 prepared pizza crust (12 inch)
⅓ cup BULL'S-EYE *or* KRAFT Original Barbecue Sauce
1 cup KRAFT 2% Milk Shredded Reduced Fat
Mozzarella Cheese
1 cup KRAFT FREE Fat Free Shredded Non-Fat
Mozzarella Cheese

SPRAY large skillet with no stick cooking spray. Add chicken, green pepper and onion; cook on medium-high heat 4 to 5 minutes or until chicken is cooked through.

PLACE crust on cookie sheet. Spread with barbecue sauce. Top with chicken mixture and cheese.

BAKE at 400°F for 15 to 18 minutes or until cheese is melted and crust is golden brown.

Makes 4 servings

Continued on page 38

Barbecue Chicken Pizza, continued

Variation: Prepare as directed, sprinkling pizza with chopped cilantro after baking.

Nutrition Information Per Serving: 540 calories, 12g total fat, 5g saturated fat, 55mg cholesterol, 1360mg sodium, 65g carbohydrate, 4g dietary fiber, 43g protein

20% daily value vitamin A, 35% daily value vitamin C, 60% daily value calcium, 25% daily value iron

Exchange: 3 Starch, 2 Vegetable, ½ Carbohydrate, 4 Meat (L)

DI GIORNO® Easy Chicken Cacciatore with Light Ravioli
Prep: 5 minutes   Cook: 10 minutes

1 package (9 ounces) DI GIORNO Light Cheese Ravioli
2 boneless skinless chicken breast halves, cut into strips
1 large green pepper, thinly sliced
1 package (15 ounces) DI GIORNO Marinara Sauce

PREPARE pasta as directed on package.

MEANWHILE, spray large nonstick skillet with no stick cooking spray. Add chicken; cook and stir on medium-high heat until cooked through. Add green pepper; cook and stir 1 minute.

STIR in sauce; cook on low heat 1 minute or until thoroughly heated. Toss with pasta. Sprinkle with DI GIORNO Shredded Parmesan Cheese, if desired.

Makes 4 servings

Nutrition Information Per Serving: 310 calories, 5g total fat, 3g saturated fat, 60mg cholesterol, 480mg sodium, 40g carbohydrate, 4g dietary fiber, 25g protein

20% daily value vitamin A, 50% daily value vitamin C

Exchange: 2 Starch, 1 Carbohydrate, 3 Meat (VL)

Simply Sensational Stir-Fry

Prep: 15 minutes   Cook: 10 minutes

¼ cup orange juice *or* apple cider vinegar
 2 tablespoons soy sauce
¼ cup oil
 1 envelope GOOD SEASONS Zesty Italian, Oriental
     Sesame *or* Honey French Salad Dressing Mix
 1 pound lean boneless beef sirloin, chicken *or* pork loin,
     cut into strips
 1 package (16 ounces) frozen mixed vegetables,
     thawed
 2½ cups hot cooked MINUTE Brown Rice

MIX juice, soy sauce, oil and salad dressing mix in cruet or small bowl as directed on envelope.

HEAT large skillet on medium-high heat. Cook meat in 1 tablespoon of the dressing mixture 4 to 5 minutes or until cooked through.

ADD vegetables and remaining dressing mixture; cook and stir until vegetables are tender-crisp. Serve over rice.

Makes 4 servings

Nutrition Information Per Serving: 490 calories, 20g total fat, 4.5g saturated fat, 55mg cholesterol, 1060mg sodium, 52g carbohydrate, 7g dietary fiber, 26g protein

10% daily value vitamin A, 30% daily value vitamin C

Exchange: 2½ Starch, 3 Vegetable, 2 Meat (L), 2 Fat

Bacon and Creamy Fettuccine

Prep: 15 minutes   **Cook:** 25 minutes

1 package (16 ounces) OSCAR MAYER Lower Sodium
    Bacon, cut into ½-inch pieces
8 ounces mushrooms, sliced
6 green onions, sliced
8 ounces fettuccine, uncooked
1 package (8 ounces) PHILADELPHIA FREE Fat Free
    Cream Cheese, cubed
⅔ cup fat-free milk
½ teaspoon garlic powder
½ teaspoon dried basil leaves, crushed
½ teaspoon dried thyme leaves, crushed
1 small tomato, chopped

COOK bacon until crisp; drain. Add mushrooms and onions to bacon in skillet; cook and stir 4 minutes. Set aside.

MEANWHILE, cook fettuccine as directed on package in large saucepan; drain. Return fettuccine to saucepan; add cream cheese, milk and seasonings. Cook and stir on medium heat until cream cheese melts.

TOSS bacon mixture with fettuccine mixture; sprinkle with tomato.

Makes 6 servings

Nutrition Information Per Serving: 330 calories, 12g total fat, 4.5g saturated fat, 30mg cholesterol, 520mg sodium, 37g carbohydrate, 2g dietary fiber, 19g protein

Exchange: 2 Starch, 1 Vegetable, 2 Meat (MF)

Bacon and Creamy Fettuccine

Cheesy Enchiladas

Prep: 15 minutes   Bake: 25 minutes

1 package (8 ounces) PHILADELPHIA FREE Fat Free
  Cream Cheese, softened
1 package (8 ounces) KRAFT FREE Fat Free Natural
  Shredded Non-Fat Cheddar Cheese, divided
¼ cup sliced green onions
6 flour tortillas (6 inch)
1 cup TACO BELL HOME ORIGINALS Thick 'N Chunky
  Salsa

BEAT cream cheese with electric mixer on medium speed
until smooth. Add 1 cup of the cheddar cheese and onions,
mixing until blended.

SPREAD ¼ cup cream cheese mixture down center of each
tortilla; roll up. Place, seam-side down, in 11×7-inch baking
dish. Pour salsa over tortillas. Sprinkle with remaining
cheddar cheese; cover.

BAKE at 350°F for 20 to 25 minutes or until thoroughly
heated.

Makes 6 servings

*Taco Bell® and Home Originals® are registered trademarks owned and
licensed by Taco Bell Corporation.*

Nutrition Information Per Serving: 210 calories, 3g total fat,
1g saturated fat, 10mg cholesterol, 1030mg sodium,
24g carbohydrate, 2g dietary fiber, 21g protein

50% daily value calcium

Exchange: 1 Starch, ½ Carbohydrate, 3 Meat (VL)

Cheesy Enchilada

Tangy Grilled Chicken Kabobs

Prep: 10 minutes plus marinating   Grill: 15 minutes

1 cup MIRACLE WHIP LIGHT Dressing
1 envelope GOOD SEASONS Italian Salad
    Dressing Mix
2 tablespoons vinegar
2 tablespoons water
1½ pounds boneless skinless chicken breast halves, cut
    into 1½-inch pieces
    Assorted cut-up fresh vegetables (peppers, mushrooms,
    onions and zucchini)

MIX dressing, salad dressing mix, vinegar and water.in cruet or small bowl. Reserve ½ cup for dipping cooked kabobs.

ARRANGE chicken and vegetables on 6 skewers. Pour remaining dressing mixture over skewers in shallow dish. Refrigerate 30 minutes to marinate. Remove kabobs from marinade; discard marinade.

PLACE kabobs on grill over medium-hot coals. Grill 10 to 15 minutes or until chicken is cooked through, turning once. Serve with reserved ½ cup dressing mixture.

Makes 6 servings

Variation: Omit grilling. Heat broiler. Place kabobs on rack of broiler pan; brush with dressing mixture. Broil 5 to 7 inches from heat 10 to 15 minutes or until chicken is cooked through.

Nutrition Information Per Serving: 240 calories, 9g total fat, 1.5g saturated fat, 55mg cholesterol, 850mg sodium, 19g carbohydrate, 3g dietary fiber, 20g protein

30% daily value vitamin A, 100% daily value vitamin C

Exchange: 2 Vegetable, ½ Carbohydrate, 2 Meat (L), 1 Fat

Tangy Grilled Chicken Kabob

Crab and Rice Primavera

Prep: 10 minutes   **Cook: 10 minutes plus standing**

2 cups frozen broccoli, cauliflower and carrot blend
¼ cup water
2 cups fat-free milk
1 package (8 ounces) imitation crabmeat
1 tablespoon butter *or* margarine
¼ teaspoon garlic powder
1½ cups MINUTE White Rice, uncooked
½ cup KRAFT FREE Nonfat Grated Topping

BRING vegetables and water to boil in medium saucepan, stirring occasionally. Reduce heat; cover and simmer 3 minutes.

ADD milk, imitation crabmeat, butter and garlic powder. Bring to boil.

STIR in rice and grated topping; cover. Remove from heat. Let stand 5 minutes. Fluff with fork.

Makes 6 servings

Nutrition Information Per Serving: 210 calories, 3.5g total fat, 2g saturated fat, 15mg cholesterol, 550mg sodium, 34g carbohydrate, 1g dietary fiber, 11g protein

70% daily value vitamin A, 20% daily value vitamin C

Exchange: 2 Starch, 1 Vegetable, 1 Meat (VL)

Easy Italian Vegetable Pasta Bake

Prep: 15 minutes   Bake: 25 minutes

3 cups mostaccioli, cooked, drained
1 jar (27½ ounces) light pasta sauce
1 package (8 ounces) KRAFT 2% Milk Shredded
    Reduced Fat Mozzarella Cheese, divided
2 cups thinly sliced mushrooms
2 cups sliced halved yellow squash
2 cups sliced halved zucchini

MIX mostaccioli, pasta sauce, 1 cup of the cheese and vegetables in large bowl.

SPOON into 13×9-inch baking dish. Top with remaining cheese.

BAKE at 375°F for 20 to 25 minutes or until thoroughly heated.

Makes 6 servings

FAT   CALCIUM

Nutrition Information Per Serving: 370 calories, 7g total fat, 4g saturated fat, 20mg cholesterol, 690mg sodium, 56g carbohydrate, 6g dietary fiber, 21g protein

35% daily value calcium

Exchange: 3 Starch, 2 Vegetable, 1 Meat (MF)

20 Minute Chicken & Brown Rice Pilaf

Prep/Cook: 20 minutes

1 tablespoon vegetable oil
4 boneless skinless chicken breast halves
1 can (10½ ounces) CAMPBELL'S® Condensed Chicken Broth
½ cup water
1 cup sliced fresh mushrooms
1 small onion, chopped
1 cup frozen peas
2 cups MINUTE Brown Rice, uncooked

HEAT oil in skillet. Add chicken; cook until browned. Remove chicken.

ADD chicken broth and water to skillet; stir. Bring to boil.

STIR in mushrooms, onion, peas and rice. Top with chicken; cover. Cook on low heat 5 minutes or until chicken is cooked through. Let stand 5 minutes.

Makes 4 servings

FAT

Nutrition Information Per Serving: 500 calories, 10g total fat, 2g saturated fat, 90mg cholesterol, 780mg sodium, 55g carbohydrate, 5g dietary fiber, 45g protein

Exchange: 3 Starch, 2 Vegetable, 5 Meat (VL), 1 Fat

20 Minute Chicken & Brown Rice Pilaf

Zesty Shrimp and Pasta

Prep: 10 minutes   Cook: 15 minutes

1 pound large shrimp, cleaned
1 cup prepared GOOD SEASONS Zesty Italian Salad
   Dressing for Fat Free Dressing, divided
2 cups sliced fresh mushrooms
1 small onion, thinly sliced
1 can (14 ounces) artichoke hearts, drained, cut into
   halves
1 tablespoon chopped fresh parsley
1 package (9 ounces) DI GIORNO Pasta, any variety,
   cooked as directed on package, drained
¼ cup KRAFT 100% Grated Parmesan Cheese

COOK and stir shrimp in ½ cup of the dressing in large
skillet on medium-high heat 2 minutes.

ADD mushrooms, onion, artichoke hearts and parsley.
Continue cooking until shrimp are pink and vegetables are
tender.

TOSS with hot cooked pasta and remaining ½ cup dressing.
Sprinkle with cheese.

Makes 6 servings

Variations: For a sophisticated variation, prepare salad dressing
mix with olive oil and balsamic vinegar.

Prepare as directed, substituting scallops for shrimp.

Prepare as directed, substituting hot cooked MINUTE White Rice for
pasta.

Nutrition Information Per Serving: 260 calories, 3.5g total fat,
1.5g saturated fat, 150mg cholesterol, 810mg sodium,
33g carbohydrate, 2g dietary fiber, 24g protein

Exchange: 2 Starch, 1 Vegetable, 2 Meat (VL)

Zesty Shrimp and Pasta

Creamy Bow Tie Primavera

Prep: 15 minutes   **Cook:** 20 minutes

8 ounces bow tie pasta, uncooked
1 cup broccoli flowerets
1 cup sliced carrots
1 package (8 ounces) PHILADELPHIA FREE Fat Free
    Cream Cheese, cubed
¾ cup fat-free milk
¼ cup KRAFT FREE Nonfat Grated Topping
¼ cup chopped green onions
½ teaspoon Italian seasoning
¼ teaspoon garlic powder

PREPARE pasta as directed on package, adding broccoli and carrots to water during last 5 minutes of cooking time. Drain.

STIR cream cheese, milk, grated topping, onions and seasonings in large saucepan on low heat until cream cheese is melted.

ADD pasta and vegetables; toss lightly.

Makes 6 servings

Nutrition Information Per Serving: 220 calories, 1.5g total fat, 1g saturated fat, 10mg cholesterol, 300mg sodium, 38g carbohydrate, 2g dietary fiber, 13g protein

100% daily value vitamin A, 25% daily value vitamin C

Exchange: 2 Starch, 1 Vegetable, 1 Meat (VL)

Stuffed Shells

Prep: 10 minutes   Bake: 40 minutes

1 container (16 ounces) BREAKSTONE'S Fat Free
    Cottage Cheese
1 package (10 ounces) frozen chopped spinach,
    thawed, well drained
1 cup KRAFT Shredded Low-Moisture Part-Skim
    Mozzarella Cheese, divided
1 medium red pepper, chopped
1 egg white
1 envelope GOOD SEASONS Italian Salad
    Dressing Mix
20 jumbo macaroni shells (for filling), cooked, drained
1 jar (13½ ounces) spaghetti sauce

MIX cottage cheese, spinach, ½ cup of the mozzarella
cheese, red pepper, egg white and salad dressing mix in
large bowl until well blended. Fill each shell with 1 heaping
tablespoon spinach mixture.

SPOON ½ of the sauce into 13×9-inch baking dish.
Arrange shells in baking dish; spoon remaining sauce over
shells. Sprinkle with remaining ½ cup mozzarella cheese.
Cover with foil.

BAKE at 400°F for 30 to 40 minutes or until thoroughly
heated.

Makes 5 servings

Nutrition Information Per Serving: 270 calories, 8g total fat,
3g saturated fat, 15mg cholesterol, 1420mg sodium,
32g carbohydrate, 5g dietary fiber, 20g protein

100% daily value vitamin A, 100% daily value vitamin C, 30% daily
value calcium

Exchange: 2 Starch, 2 Meat (L)

Diabetic Choices

On the Sidelines

Make your meals special with this exciting medley of salads and side dishes.

Italian Green Beans

Prep: 5 minutes   Cook: 10 minutes

½ cup water
 1 package (16 ounces) frozen whole green beans
½ cup cubed POLLY-O Non-Fat Mozzarella Cheese
       (¼-inch cubes)
½ cup chopped seeded tomato
⅓ cup KRAFT FREE Italian Fat Free Dressing

BRING water to boil in medium saucepan. Add green beans; cook 2 minutes or until tender. Drain.

STIR in cheese, tomato and dressing. Serve hot.

Makes 6 servings

Nutrition Information Per Serving: 50 calories, 0g total fat, 0g saturated fat, 0mg cholesterol, 300mg sodium, 7g carbohydrate, 3g dietary fiber, 5g protein

10% daily value vitamin A, 15% daily value vitamin C

Exchange: 2 Vegetable

Roasted Potato and Vegetable Salad

Prep: 10 minutes   Bake: 45 minutes

2 pounds red potatoes, cubed
2 zucchini, thinly sliced lengthwise
2 carrots, diagonally sliced
1 small red onion, cut into wedges
2 cups KRAFT TASTE OF LIFE Tomato & Garlic Dressing

TOSS vegetables with dressing in large bowl.

SPOON into shallow roasting pan.

BAKE at 400°F for 40 to 45 minutes or until vegetables are tender, stirring occasionally.

Makes 8 servings

Nutrition Information Per Serving: 230 calories, 10g total fat, 1g saturated fat, 0mg cholesterol, 500mg sodium, 32g carbohydrate, 4g dietary fiber, 4g protein

100% daily value vitamin A, 40% daily value vitamin C, 100% daily value vitamin E

Exchange: 1½ Starch, 1 Vegetable, 2 Fat

Roasted Potato and Vegetable Salad

Broccoli & Carrot Salad

Prep: 15 minutes plus refrigerating

    1 pound broccoli flowerets
    2 cups sliced mushrooms
    1 carrot, shredded
    ½ cup sliced green onions
    1 cup KRAFT TASTE OF LIFE Country Ranch Dressing
    ¼ cup dry-roasted sunflower seeds

TOSS broccoli, mushrooms, carrot and onions with dressing; cover. Refrigerate.

SPRINKLE with sunflower seeds just before serving.

Makes 8 servings

Nutrition Information Per Serving: 110 calories, 7g total fat, 0.5g saturated fat, 0mg cholesterol, 290mg sodium, 11g carbohydrate, 3g dietary fiber, 3g protein

70% daily value vitamin A, 90% daily value vitamin C, 60% daily value vitamin E, 15% daily value folic acid

Exchange: 2 Vegetable, 1½ Fat

Honey Dijon Asparagus

Prep: 5 minutes   Cook: 5 minutes

    1½ cups water
    24 thin asparagus spears, ends trimmed
    ⅓ cup KRAFT FREE Honey Dijon Fat Free Dressing

BRING water to boil in large saucepan. Add asparagus; cook 5 minutes or until tender-crisp. Drain.

POUR dressing over asparagus; toss to coat. Serve immediately.

Makes 4 servings

KRAFT® TASTE OF LIFE™ Salad

Prep: 15 minutes

5 cups torn romaine lettuce
4 cups torn spinach
1 can (15 ounces) red kidney beans, rinsed, drained
1 cup broccoli flowerets
1 cup sliced carrots
1 red or green pepper, cut into thin strips
1 tomato, cut into wedges
¼ cup slivered red onion
¾ cup KRAFT TASTE OF LIFE Tomato & Garlic Dressing

TOSS all ingredients in large bowl.

Makes 6 servings

FIBER

Spinach & Orange Salad
Prep: 20 minutes

10 cups torn spinach

2 cups fresh orange sections

½ cup sliced red onion

1 package (4 ounces) ATHENOS Crumbled Feta Cheese

1 cup prepared GOOD SEASONS Italian Salad Dressing for Fat Free Dressing

TOSS spinach, oranges, onion and cheese in large bowl.

ADD dressing; toss lightly.

Makes 10 servings

Variations: Prepare as directed, substituting 2 cans (11 ounces each) mandarin orange segments, drained, for fresh orange sections.

Prepare as directed, adding ¼ cup toasted slivered almonds.

Nutrition Information Per Serving: 70 calories, 2.5g total fat, 1.5g saturated fat, 5mg cholesterol, 330mg sodium, 8g carbohydrate, 2g dietary fiber, 3g protein

40% daily value vitamin A, 45% daily value vitamin C

Exchange: ½ Fruit, 1 Vegetable, ½ Fat

Spinach & Orange Salad

Pear & Raspberry Salad

Prep: 20 minutes

2 pears, thinly sliced
1 package (10 ounces) salad greens
½ cup SEVEN SEAS FREE Raspberry Vinaigrette Fat Free Dressing
½ cup ATHENOS Crumbled Feta Cheese
¼ cup chopped toasted pecans

TOSS pears and greens in large bowl.

ADD remaining ingredients; toss lightly.

Makes 8 servings

Nutrition Information Per Serving: 100 calories, 5g total fat, 2g saturated fat, 5mg cholesterol, 240mg sodium, 12g carbohydrate, 2g dietary fiber, 3g protein

25% daily value vitamin A, 15% daily value vitamin C

Exchange: ½ Fruit, 1 Vegetable, 1 Fat

Creamy Cucumber Salad

Prep: 15 minutes

2 cucumbers, thinly sliced
2 plum tomatoes, diced
½ cup thin sweet onion slices
½ cup KRAFT TASTE OF LIFE Country Ranch Dressing
2 tablespoons chopped toasted pecans

TOSS cucumbers, tomatoes and onion with dressing.

SPRINKLE with pecans just before serving.

Makes 4 servings

Italian Vegetable Salad
Prep: 10 minutes plus refrigerating

1 package (9 ounces) DI GIORNO Three Cheese
    Tortellini, cooked, drained
1 small zucchini, cut in half lengthwise, sliced
½ *each* green and red pepper, chopped
½ cup halved cherry tomatoes
½ cup prepared GOOD SEASONS Reduced Calorie
    Italian *or* Zesty Italian Salad Dressing
2 green onions, diagonally sliced

TOSS all ingredients in large bowl; cover. Refrigerate at least 2 hours.

STIR in additional dressing just before serving, if desired.

Makes 8 servings

Quick Italian Spinach Pie

Prep: 10 minutes   Bake: 40 minutes

1 container (16 ounces) BREAKSTONE'S *or* KNUDSEN
    2% Cottage Cheese
1 package (10 ounces) frozen chopped spinach,
    thawed, well drained
1 cup KRAFT Shredded Low-Moisture Part-Skim
    Mozzarella Cheese
4 eggs, beaten
1 jar (7 ounces) roasted red peppers, well drained,
    chopped
⅓ cup KRAFT 100% Grated Parmesan Cheese
1 teaspoon dried oregano leaves

MIX all ingredients.

POUR into greased 9-inch pie plate.

BAKE at 350°F for 40 minutes or until center is set.

Makes 8 servings

Variation: Prepare as directed, substituting ½ cup chopped red pepper for roasted red pepper.

CALCIUM

Nutrition Information Per Serving: 150 calories, 8g total fat, 4g saturated fat, 125mg cholesterol, 450mg sodium, 6g carbohydrate, 1g dietary fiber, 15g protein

50% daily value vitamin A, 25% daily value calcium

Exchange: 1 Vegetable, 2 Meat (L)

Quick Italian Spinach Pie

Diabetic Choices

Drinks on the House

This collection of thirst-quenching hot and cold beverages is sure to please young and old alike.

Fizzy Cran-Grape Lemonade Punch

Prep: 10 minutes

1 envelope KOOL-AID Sugar Free Lemonade Flavor Low Calorie Soft Drink Mix
1 bottle (48 ounces) chilled reduced-calorie cranberry-grape juice cocktail
1 bottle (1 liter) chilled seltzer
1 navel orange, sliced, cut into quarters
Ice cubes *or* crushed ice

PLACE drink mix in large plastic or glass pitcher. Add cranberry-grape juice cocktail; stir to dissolve. Refrigerate.

POUR into large punch bowl just before serving. Stir in seltzer and oranges. Serve over ice.

Makes 2½ quarts or 10 (1-cup) servings

Nutrition Information Per Serving: 35 calories, 0g total fat, 0g saturated fat, 0mg cholesterol, 50mg sodium, 7g carbohydrate, 0g dietary fiber, less than 1g protein

90% daily value vitamin C

Exchange: ½ Fruit

66

Hot Spiced Tea

Prep: 10 minutes

1 tub CRYSTAL LIGHT Iced Tea Mix *or* CRYSTAL LIGHT
    Peach Flavor Iced Tea Mix *or* CRYSTAL LIGHT
    Raspberry Flavor Iced Tea Mix
1 tub CRYSTAL LIGHT Lemonade Flavor Low Calorie Soft
    Drink Mix
1 teaspoon ground cinnamon
⅛ to ¼ teaspoon ground cloves

MIX drink mixes and spices. Store in tightly covered jar.

Makes about 8 teaspoons or 16 servings

To Make 1 Quart: Measure 3 level teaspoons mix into heatproof
pitcher or bowl. Add 1 quart boiling water; stir to dissolve mix.

For Single Serving: Measure ½ level teaspoon mix into cup. Add
¾ cup (6 ounces) boiling water; stir to dissolve mix.

Nutrition Information Per Serving: 5 calories, 0g total fat, 0g
saturated fat, 0mg cholesterol, 5mg sodium, 0g carbohydrate, 0g
dietary fiber, 0g protein

Exchange: Free

Hot Spiced Tea

COUNTRY TIME® Lemon Berry Cooler

Prep: 5 minutes

1 cup prepared COUNTRY TIME Lemonade Flavor
Sugar Free Low Calorie Drink Mix
½ cup cold 2% reduced-fat milk
½ cup strawberry *or* raspberry sorbet or sherbet
½ cup ice cubes *or* crushed ice

PLACE all ingredients in blender container; cover. Blend on high speed until smooth. Serve immediately.

Makes 2 (1-cup) servings

FAT   CALCIUM

Nutrition Information Per Serving: 100 calories, 2g total fat, 1.5g saturated fat, 10mg cholesterol, 60mg sodium, 18g carbohydrate, 0g dietary fiber, 3g protein

10% daily value calcium

Exchange: 1 Carbohydrate, ½ Fat

Top to bottom: COUNTRY TIME® Lemon Berry Cooler, COUNTRY TIME® Lemon Creamy Frosty (page 72)

Sunny Orange Delight

Prep: 10 minutes plus refrigerating

1 envelope KOOL-AID Sugar Free Lemonade Flavor Low
    Calorie Soft Drink Mix
8 cups (2 quarts) cold water
1 can (6 ounces) frozen orange juice concentrate,
    thawed
    Ice cubes

PLACE drink mix in large plastic or glass pitcher. Add water;
stir to dissolve. Stir in juice concentrate. Refrigerate. Serve
over ice.

Makes 8 (1-cup) servings

Nutrition Information Per Serving: 45 calories, 0g total fat,
0g saturated fat, 0mg cholesterol, 10mg sodium, 11g carbohydrate,
0g dietary fiber, less than 1g protein

70% daily value vitamin C

Exchange: 1 Fruit

COUNTRY TIME® Lemon Creamy Frosty

Prep: 5 minutes

1 cup prepared COUNTRY TIME Lemonade Flavor
    Sugar Free Low Calorie Drink Mix
1 cup no-sugar-added vanilla ice cream
½ cup ice cubes *or* crushed ice

PLACE all ingredients in blender container; cover. Blend on
high speed about 30 seconds or until thickened and
smooth. Serve immediately.

Makes 2 (1-cup) servings

Tropical Coffee Shake

Prep: 10 minutes

½ cup cold fat-free milk
⅓ cup GENERAL FOODS INTERNATIONAL COFFEES
    Sugar Free Fat Free, French Vanilla Cafe Flavor
1 can (8 ounces) crushed pineapple in juice, drained
1 small ripe banana
2 cups fat-free no-sugar-added vanilla ice cream,
    softened

PLACE milk, flavored instant coffee, pineapple, banana and ice cream in blender container; cover.

BLEND on high speed until smooth. Garnish with COOL WHIP Whipped Topping and toasted coconut, if desired.

Makes 4 (1-cup) servings

FAT   CALCIUM

Nutrition Information Per Serving: 180 calories, 1g total fat, 0g saturated fat, 0mg cholesterol, 125mg sodium, 40g carbohydrate, 1g dietary fiber, 5g protein

10% daily value vitamin C, 10% daily value calcium

Exchange: 2½ Carbohydrate

Sunrise Punch

Prep: 5 minutes plus refrigerating

1 tub CRYSTAL LIGHT TROPICAL PASSIONS Strawberry
Kiwi Flavor Low Calorie Soft Drink Mix
2 cups cold water
2 cups chilled unsweetened pineapple juice
1 bottle (1 liter) chilled seltzer
Ice cubes

PLACE drink mix in large plastic or glass pitcher. Add water
and juice; stir to dissolve. Refrigerate.

JUST before serving, pour into large punch bowl. Stir in
seltzer. Serve over ice.

Makes 2 quarts or 8 (1-cup) servings

Nutrition Information Per Serving: 40 calories, 0g total fat,
0g saturated fat, 0mg cholesterol, 5mg sodium, 9g carbohydrate,
0g dietary fiber, 0g protein

10% daily value vitamin C

Exchange: ½ Fruit

Sunrise Punch

Cool Yogurt Smoothie

Prep: 5 minutes

1 container (8 ounces) BREYERS Lowfat Yogurt, any flavor

2½ cups thawed COOL WHIP FREE Whipped Topping, divided

2 cups fresh or frozen strawberries *or* any other seasonal fruit, chopped

2 cups ice cubes

PLACE yogurt, 1½ cups of the whipped topping, fruit and ice in blender container; cover. Blend until smooth. Top each serving with ¼ cup of the remaining whipped topping. Serve immediately.

Makes 4 (1-cup) servings

Breyers® is a registered trademark of Unilever, N.V., used under license.

Nutrition Information Per Serving: 110 calories, 2g total fat, 1.5g saturated fat, less than 5mg cholesterol, 40mg sodium, 23g carbohydrate, 2g dietary fiber, 3g protein

90% daily value vitamin C

Exchange: 1½ Carbohydrate

Top to bottom: Cool Yogurt Smoothie, Tropical Coffee Shake (page 73)

Diabetic Choices

Sweet Treats

Finally, here is an awesome array of dessert and snack recipes that are easy to prepare and fun to share.

Strawberry Short Cut

Prep: 10 minutes

1 package (13.6 ounces) fat-free pound cake
3 cups strawberries, sliced, sweetened
3¼ cups thawed COOL WHIP LITE Whipped Topping

CUT cake into 16 slices. Place 8 of the cake slices on individual dessert plates.

SPOON about 3 tablespoons of the strawberries over each cake slice. Top each with ¼ cup whipped topping. Repeat layers, ending with whipped topping. Serve immediately.

Makes 8 servings

FAT

Nutrition Information Per Serving: 270 calories, 2g total fat, 1.5g saturated fat, 0mg cholesterol, 170mg sodium, 64g carbohydrate, 3g dietary fiber, 3g protein

70% daily value vitamin C

Exchange: 4 Carbohydrate

Lemon Mousse with Raspberry Sauce

Prep: 5 minutes plus refrigerating

1 ½ cups boiling water
  1 package (8-serving size) *or* 2 packages
    (4-serving size each) JELL-O Brand Lemon Flavor
    Sugar Free Low Calorie Gelatin
  2 teaspoons grated lemon peel
  1 cup cold apple juice
    Ice cubes
  1 tub (8 ounces) COOL WHIP FREE Whipped Topping,
    thawed
  1 package (10 ounces) frozen raspberries *or*
    strawberries, thawed, puréed in blender

STIR boiling water into gelatin and lemon peel in large bowl at least 2 minutes until gelatin is completely dissolved. Mix apple juice and ice to measure 1¾ cups. Add to gelatin, stirring until slightly thickened. Remove any remaining ice.

STIR in whipped topping with wire whisk. Pour into serving bowl or 10 dessert dishes.

REFRIGERATE 4 hours or until firm. Serve with raspberry sauce.

Makes 10 servings

FAT

Nutrition Information Per Serving: 80 calories, 1.5g total fat, 1g saturated fat, 0mg cholesterol, 60mg sodium, 15g carbohydrate, 2g dietary fiber, 2g protein

10% daily value vitamin C

Exchange: 1 Carbohydrate

Bran Fruit and Nut Cookies

Prep: 15 minutes   **Bake:** 10 minutes

½ cup firmly packed brown sugar
¼ cup oil
2 tablespoons water
2 egg whites, slightly beaten
1 teaspoon ground cinnamon
½ teaspoon baking soda
⅛ teaspoon salt
1 cup flour
1½ cups POST Raisin Bran Cereal
¼ cup chopped walnuts
¼ cup chopped dried apricots (optional)

MIX sugar, oil, water, egg whites, cinnamon, baking soda and salt in large bowl. Stir in flour and cereal. Mix in walnuts and apricots.

DROP by rounded teaspoons onto lightly greased cookie sheets.

BAKE at 350°F for 10 minutes or until browned. Remove and cool on wire racks. Store in tightly covered container.

Makes 4 dozen

Nutrition Information Per Serving (3 cookies): 130 calories, 5g total fat, 0.5g saturated fat, 0mg cholesterol, 115mg sodium, 20g carbohydrate, 1g dietary fiber, 2g protein

Exchange: 1 Carbohydrate, 1 Fat

Banana Cinnamon Spice Pie

Prep: 10 minutes plus refrigerating

1 large ripe banana, sliced
1 prepared reduced-fat graham cracker crumb crust
    (6 ounce *or* 9 inch)
1½ cups cold fat-free milk
  2 packages (4-serving size each) JELL-O White
    Chocolate *or* Vanilla Flavor Fat Free Sugar Free
    Instant Reduced Calorie Pudding & Pie Filling
½ teaspoon ground cinnamon
  1 tub (8 ounces) COOL WHIP FREE Whipped Topping,
    thawed

PLACE banana slices in bottom of crust.

POUR milk into large bowl. Add pudding mixes and cinnamon. Beat with wire whisk 1 minute. Gently stir in whipped topping. Spoon into crust. Sprinkle with additional cinnamon, if desired.

REFRIGERATE 4 hours or until set.

Makes 8 servings

Nutrition Information Per Serving: 210 calories, 5g total fat, 2.5g saturated fat, 0mg cholesterol, 460mg sodium, 38g carbohydrate, 1g dietary fiber, 3g protein

Exchange: 2½ Carbohydrate, ½ Fat